Animal Disguises

KINGFISHER

Published in 2010 by Kingfisher
an imprint of Macmillan Children's Books
a division of Macmillan Publishers Limited
20 New Wharf Road
London N1 9RR
Basingstoke and Oxford
Associated companies throughout the world
www.panmacmillan.com

ISBN 978-0-7534-3004-0

First published as *Kingfisher Young Knowledge: Animal Disguises* in 2004
Additional material produced for Macmillan Children's Books by Discovery Books Ltd

1 3 5 7 9 8 6 4 2

1TR/0410/WKT/UNTD/140MA/C

A CIP catalogue record for this book is available from the British Library.

Printed in China

Note to readers: the website addresses listed in this book are correct at
the time of going to print. However, due to the ever-changing nature
of the internet, website addresses and content can change. Websites
can contain links that are unsuitable for children. The publisher cannot
be held responsible for changes in website addresses or content, or
for information obtained through a third party. We strongly advise
that internet searches should be supervised by an adult.

Acknowledgements

The publishers would like to thank the following for permission to reproduce their material. Every care has been taken
to trace copyright holders. However, if there have been unintentional omissions or failure to trace copyright holders,
we apologize and will, if informed, endeavour to make corrections in any future edition.
b = bottom, *c* = centre, *l* = left, *t* = top, *r* = right

Cover main Shutterstock/Kristina Postnikova; cover *l* Shutterstock/Sergey Khachatryan; cover *r* Shutterstock/Olga Utlyakova; page 1 Ardea;
3 Naturepl; 4–5 Naturepl; 7 Naturepl; 8*b* Getty Images (Getty); 9*t* Oxford Scientific Films (OSF); 10–11 Ardea; 11*t* Ardea; 11*b* Corbis; 12 Nature
History Picture Agency (NHPA); 13*tr* Getty; 13*cl* OSF; 13*b* Corbis; 14*cl* OSF; 14*b* OSF; 15*tr* Fogden Photographs; 15*b* Naturepl; 16*tr* Ardea; 16*b* OSF;
17 Fogden Photographs; 18–19 Naturepl; 18*tl* Naturepl; 19*tr* Fogden Photographs; 20–21 Corbis; 20*b* Ardea; 21*br* Ardea; 22–23 National Geographic
Image Collection; 22*cl* NHPA; 23*tr* OSF; 24–25 National Geographic Image Collection; 24*bl* Ardea; 24*br* Ardea; 26*b* OSF; 27*t* Naturepl; 27*b* Naturepl;
28*cr* Fogden Photographs; 28*bl* OSF; 29*tr* OSF; 29*b* Corbis; 30*tl* Ardea; 30*b* Ardea; 31*t* Ardea; 31*br* Ardea; 32–33 Getty; 32*bl* Fainting Goat Association,
USA; 33*tr* National Geographic Image Collection; 34*t* Ardea; 34*b* Corbis; 35 Ardea; 36–37 Ardea; 36*bl* OSF; 37*tr* Naturepl; 38–39 Ardea; 38*bl* Ardea;
39*tl* NHPA; 39*tr* NHPA; 39*b* Ardea; 40 Corbis; 41 Naturepl; 41*t* Corbis; 48*c* Shutterstock Images/Eric Isselee; 48*b* Shutterstock Images/Ostill;
49*t* Shutterstock Images/Lori Froeb; 49*b* Shutterstock Images/Ecoprint; 52*t* Shutterstock Images/Grant Terry; 52*l* Shutterstock Images/Sam
Chadwick; 53*l* Shutterstock Images/John Swanepoel; 53*b* Shutterstock Images/Iarus; 56 Shutterstock Images/Kristian Sekulic

Commissioned photography on pages 42–47 by Andy Crawford
Thank you to models Anastasia Mitchell, Holly Hadaway, Sonnie Nash

discover science

Animal Disguises

Belinda Weber

KINGFISHER

Contents

What is camouflage?

Camouflage is the way an animal blends in with its surroundings. It can be the animal's body shape, or the colour of its coat or skin that helps it match its home. Camouflage is used for two reasons – to hunt, or to hide from predators.

Silent power

Creeping through the undergrowth, a tiger is difficult to see. The long grass is light in colour, but its shadow looks black. The light and dark lines blend in with markings on the tiger's back.

Spots and stripes

Spots and stripes break up an animal's shape. At dusk or dawn, when many creatures feed, their markings blend in with shadows, making it difficult to see each animal clearly.

Who's who?

A zebra's coat confuses predators. All the stripes merge and it is hard to see where one zebra ends and another begins.

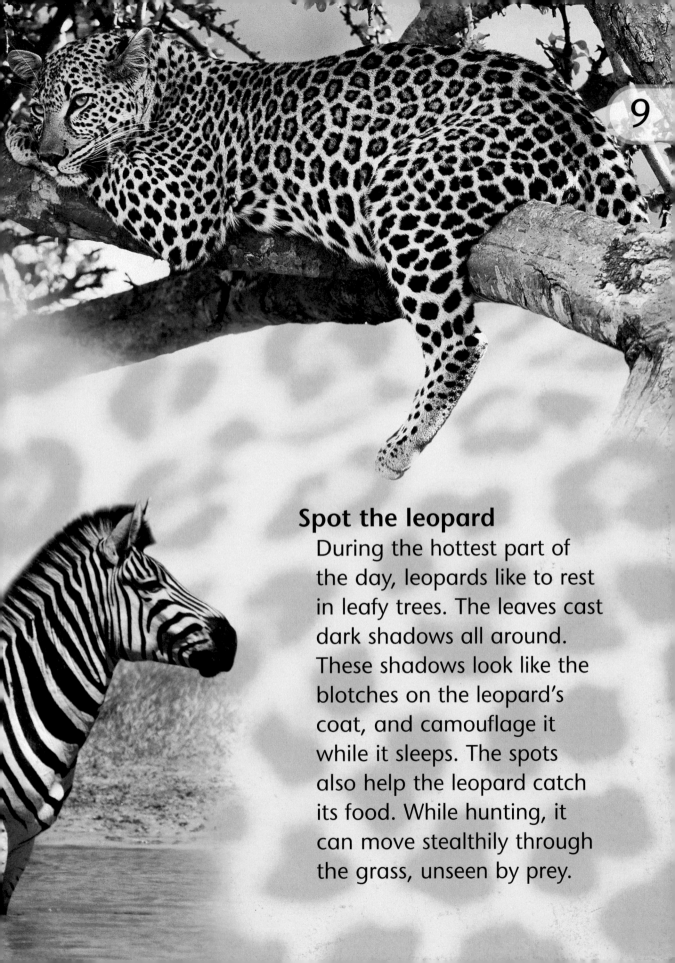

Spot the leopard

During the hottest part of the day, leopards like to rest in leafy trees. The leaves cast dark shadows all around. These shadows look like the blotches on the leopard's coat, and camouflage it while it sleeps. The spots also help the leopard catch its food. While hunting, it can move stealthily through the grass, unseen by prey.

Blending in

Bold colours and shapes are great disguises. In wooded areas, where there is a lot of light and shade, bold markings make it hard to see what is a shadow and what is an animal.

Standing tall
The dark splodges on a giraffe's coat look like patches of shade. They help disguise it as it feeds in the acacia trees in its African habitat.

Safe in the grass

When it is first born, a baby red deer cannot run fast enough to keep up with its mother. She hides it in grasses where its spotty brown coat matches the light and shadows on the ground.

Humbug stripes

Tapirs live in rainforests. For the first six months of their lives, baby tapirs have a stripey coat that makes them hard to see in dappled jungle light.

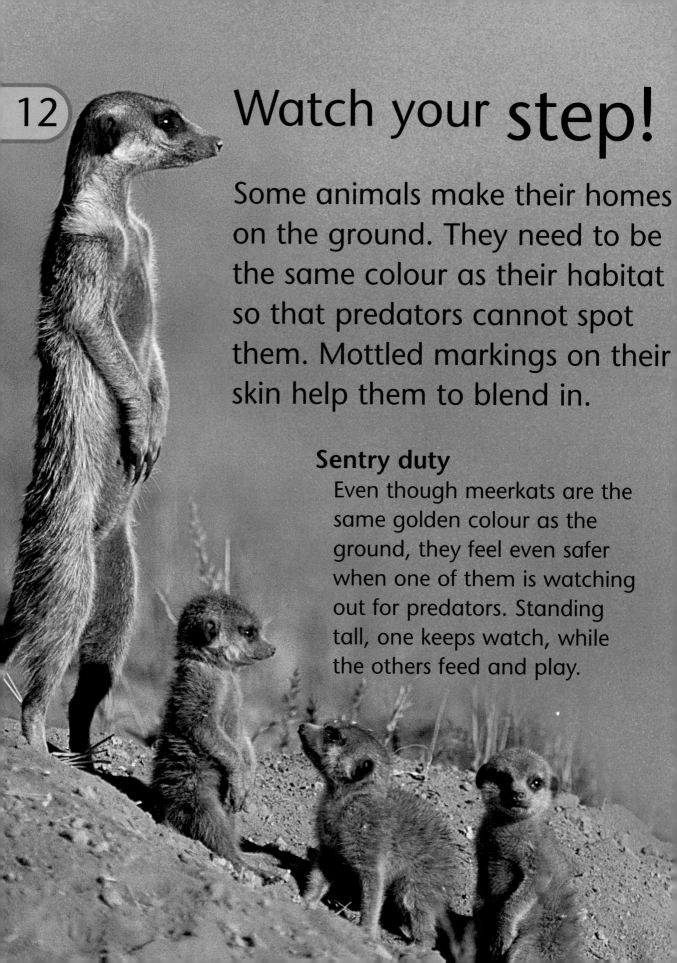

Watch your step!

Some animals make their homes on the ground. They need to be the same colour as their habitat so that predators cannot spot them. Mottled markings on their skin help them to blend in.

Sentry duty

Even though meerkats are the same golden colour as the ground, they feel even safer when one of them is watching out for predators. Standing tall, one keeps watch, while the others feed and play.

Living carpets

Carpet sharks look like the seabed. This is because the blotchy patches on their skin match the rocks and stones around them.

In hiding

Pheasants' feathers are multi-coloured, so it is hard to see them in shady light. They hide in wooded areas or in long grass.

Froggy floors

Marsupial frogs live among the fallen leaves in rainforests. Their brown, patchy skin makes them difficult to see. Even the babies look like the forest floor.

Life in a leaf

Leaves make good hiding places. Some animals hide there to catch prey by surprise. Others eat the leaves and do not want to be seen by predators.

Leafy looks

The body, legs and head of this wandering leaf insect are shaped just like the leaves it eats.

Dead ringer

The leaf-tailed gecko scuttles about the forest floor. Its body shape and colour make it look like dead leaves.

Life on the river bed

The Surinam toad blends in perfectly with the leaves that blanket the river bed, where it lives. It hides, camouflaged, waiting for passing prey.

Lacy lichen

Lichen katydids live in tropical cloud forests. They merge almost seamlessly with the lichen plants that grow there. The feathery leaves of the plant match the lacy pattern on the katydid's body.

Flowers and fruit

Plants often have bright flowers and tasty fruit. They need animals to help them spread their seeds. But even the prettiest flower is not always what it seems.

Pretty in pink

Lurking in this bright pink flower, a crab spider waits for a tasty meal. It holds its front legs wide apart, ready to grab its prey.

Watch out!

Hidden among the white flowers, this orchid mantis is difficult to see. If an insect flies by, the mantis will attack and eat the welcome snack.

Fruit surprise
These tasty-looking palm fruits hide a deadly secret. Waiting silently among the fruit, an eyelash viper hopes its prey will come within easy striking distance.

Stony features

A huge number of creatures live among rocks and pebbles. The different colours of the stones and the shadows they cast make great hiding places.

Stone home

An African rock python is hard to see among the stones. Its skin is mottled, so it matches the colours of the rocks perfectly. It rests on the stones while it warms itself in the sun, then slides off quietly in search of prey.

Jumping stones

Stone grasshoppers are so good at their disguise that they are often only visible when they move. Their long back legs allow them to make powerful jumps, so they can leap away from predators.

Star spotting

The stargazer fish buries itself in the seabed to complete its camouflage. The only things that give it away are its eyes and mouth, but even these look like pebbles and sand. Fish that swim too close are snapped up for a tasty meal.

Like a branch

Many animals try to look like sticks to fool predators. Others take the shape of branches and hide in trees. Some predators, such as crocodiles, hope to pass as tree trunks so their food will not notice them.

Log alike

Floating on the surface of a river, a crocodile looks just like a log. Its unlucky prey gets a nasty shock when it pauses for a drink!

Walking sticks

With its long, thin body
and legs, a stick insect
is easily confused with
a twig. It even sways
gently in the wind, so
it looks just right.

Slowly, slowly

Clinging upside down to
branches, sloths creep
around their forest homes.
When it rains, algae grow
on the branches and in
the sloth's fur, helping
it hide in the trees.

Above and **below**

Some animals have light tummies and dark backs. This is a double disguise, called countershading. It makes them hard to see from above and from below.

Light and dark

The lapwing has a dark grey-green back that blends in with grass. This makes it tricky to see from the air. But when it flies, the lapwing's white tummy blends in with the light sky, so it is difficult to see from the ground.

Black and white

When it swims,
a penguin's white
tummy merges with
the lighter surface water.
From above, its dark back
looks like deep water.

Sneaky sharks

Sharks and other fish use countershading as
well. A shark is able to sneak up on a shoal
of fish from above or below, as its dark and
light colouring helps break up its shape.

New season's colours

Camouflage works only if the animal looks like its surroundings. When the weather changes, some animals have to change their coats so that they still look the same as their habitat.

The latest look

Snowshoe hares live in Alaska, USA. In summer, their coats are brown to blend in with the ground. In winter, the hares grow a new, white coat to help them stay hidden in the snow.

A new winter coat

Arctic foxes are predators and need to be able to creep up on their prey. In winter, their snowy white coats blend in perfectly with their icy world. In summer, their coats are brown, so they match the earthy colours of the season.

All change

Chameleons are the masters of disguise. Special cells in their skin let them change their skin colour to match their backgrounds. Some chameleons can switch colours in under 20 seconds.

parson's chameleon

antsingy leaf chameleon

Colourful creatures

Chameleons are predators and need
to stay hidden until they attack their
insect prey. Whether resting in
leaves or hunting in the desert,
a chameleon can change its skin
colour to fit the background.

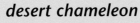

desert chameleon

Shape shifters

Sometimes, skin colour and shape are not enough to keep an animal hidden. Sticks, stones, plants and even clothes may be used to make a new disguise.

Living garden

Darkling beetles cover their bodies with lichen and other small plants. These grow and help the beetle stay hidden from predators as it searches for food.

Crafty weaver

The clothes moth larva does not like to be disturbed whilst feeding. It fashions itself a coat out of whichever jumper it is eating, and then feasts without interruption!

Making a shell suit

A caddis fly larva's disguise is a case that grows around its body. On this clever camouflage, the larva sticks shells, small pebbles, leaves or any other small items it can find.

Hanging decorations

A decorator crab's body is covered with tiny hooked hairs. It hangs seaweed from these hairs to help it hide on the seabed.

Eye disguises

An animal's eyes are very sensitive. If they are attacked, it can cause blindness and put the creature's life in danger. For this reason, some animals have 'false eyes'. Others hide their eyes in bold patterns.

Eyes down

Fruit bats like this one (above) rest in big groups and often squabble. To protect their eyes during fights, they have white tufts beneath their ears. Attackers go for these instead of the real eyes.

Heads or tails?

The eyes of butterfly fish are hidden in a dark stripe across their faces. They also have a false eye near the tail, so predators go for the wrong end.

How many eyes?

The eyespots on this emperor moth's wings look like eyes. If a predator attacks them, it is unlikely to do much harm and the moth can escape.

Looking back

This pearl-spotted owlet has false eyes, made from dark feathers, on the back of its head. These decoy eyes may confuse both predators and prey about which way the owl is looking.

Playing tricks

Some animals have an extra defence when attacked. They behave strangely or do something unexpected that confuses the predator and stops it attacking.

All fall down

Fainting goats perform a nifty trick when they feel threatened – they fall over in a dead faint! Once the danger has passed, the goat gets up and carries on.

deflated balloon fish

Spiky mouthful

Balloon fish look like
a small, tasty bite when
swimming normally, with
flattened spines. But as
soon as they are in any
danger, they gulp down
water to blow themselves
up into a big spiky ball.
This makes them look far
less mouth-watering!

inflated balloon fish

Surprise!

Sometimes a predator is put off eating an animal if it is startled in some way. Many animals rely on surprising their attacker and then they escape.

Which way round?

The shingleback lizard's tail looks like its head! Attackers which mistakenly go for the tail find the lizard shoots off in the other direction.

Flashing red

At rest, a fire-bellied toad looks like floating pondweed. But when startled, it rears up and flashes its red and black belly.

Frilling

A frilled lizard has a flap
of skin around its neck
that opens like an
umbrella when
it is scared.

Terrible traps

Some predators are so well disguised that prey comes close, unaware of any risk. Others bring their prey within striking distance using a trap or lure.

Wagging tongues

The pink tip of this alligator snapping turtle's tongue wriggles like a worm. If a fish swims up to eat the worm, it becomes the turtle's dinner!

Tempting tails

The yellow end of a copperhead snake's tail looks like lunch to a frog. But if it gets too close, the frog itself ends up on the menu.

End of the line

Anglerfish live in deep, dark oceans. They lure prey with a 'fishing line' that hangs over their mouths. The end of the line glows. Fish come to look at the light and are eaten by the crafty anglers.

Clever copies

Predators learn what tastes bad or is poisonous, and avoid it. Some prey animals mimic, or copy, nasty-tasting objects or animals. Predators then steer clear of them too.

No sting in the tail!

Bees, wasps and hornets have painful stings and so predators avoid them. This clearwing moth looks like a hornet and this keeps it safe from predators.

Copy ant

Ants produce a poison to stop attackers. The mirid bug looks like an ant and this protects it.

*Pueblan
milk snake*

*Eastern
coral snake*

Mix up

Coral snakes are highly venomous.
Milk snakes are harmless, but look
like the coral snakes. This means that
most attackers leave them both alone.

Not what it seems

Some predators are clever
mimics. This praying mantis
looks like a bird dropping!
If an insect comes close, it
soon gets snapped up.

Hide and seek babies

Baby animals are often left alone while the parents go to find food. To keep them safe, their colourings blend in with their surroundings.

Sitting pretty

Lion cubs have sandy coloured coats that match their savannah home. They hide in the grass while their mum is away.

Hard to spot

Arctic tern chicks wait for their parents to bring them food. Their feathers look like the surrounding rocks, allowing them to blend in. The little chick beside the chirpy one shows just how good this camouflage is.

Snow babies

Harp seal cubs live in icy places. Their white coats help them to hide on the snowy ground until they are big enough to defend themselves.

Make a caddis fly larva's house

Caddis fly larvae live underwater. They make a camouflaged case in which to live. The case is made out of whatever they can find in the pond or stream where they live. They carry the case around with them, and hope no-one will notice them. Make a disguised home for a model caddis fly larva.

You will need
- Cardboard tube
- Brown paint
- Paintbrush
- Glue
- Camouflage material: twigs, leaves, shells, stones
- Modelling dough – 3 colours
- 1 yellow pipe cleaner

Mix some brown paint and water. Take the cardboard tube and paint it brown. Leave it to dry. This is your caddis fly larva's case.

Glue small twigs, dried leaves, shells and small stones on to the cardboard tube. Make sure the tube is well covered. Leave to dry.

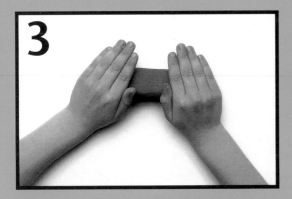

3

Roll some blue modelling dough into a sausage shape. Make sure it is small enough to fit inside the tube. This is the larva's body.

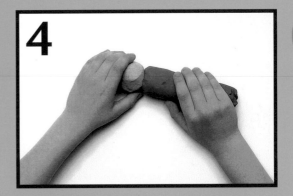

4

Take a smaller piece of light blue modelling dough and roll it into a ball. Attach it to the darker blue body. Your larva now has a head!

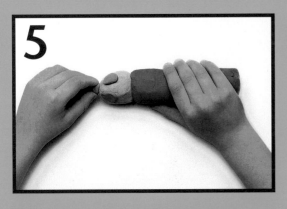

5

With some green modelling dough, make two tiny flat balls for the eyes and a small cone for the mouth.

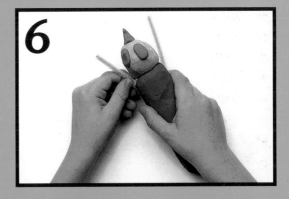

6

Cut a pipe cleaner in half and push each piece into either side of the body. The larva is now ready to be put inside its new home.

Tiger fun

Tiger face painting

Paint your own face, looking in a mirror. Or, draw tiger stripes on a friend's face and then ask them to paint yours.

You will need
- Face paints and brush
- Sponge
- Warm water
- Soap

Start with a clean face! Put black face paint on a brush. Colour in the tip of your nose and your lips. Draw a stripe beneath your nose.

With white paint, draw whiskers coming out from under your nose, across your cheeks and around the corners of your mouth.

Paint black stripes under your eyes and on your forehead, chin and cheeks. Add white stripes on your eyebrows and a dot on your nose.

4

Use red and orange paints to fill in some lines on your cheeks, chin and forehead.

Add the finishing touches with some gold paint on your forehead, cheeks and chin. Now that you have got the tiger look, it is time to test the disguise. How many people recognize you with a tiger's face?

When you have had enough of being a tiger, carefully wash off the face paints using warm water, soap and a sponge.

Mystery picture

Draw a camouflage picture

Chameleons are masters of disguise and these two are no exception. In this clever two-in-one picture, you will need two outlines of a chameleon. To get the basic shape, you could trace around the parson's chameleon on page 27.

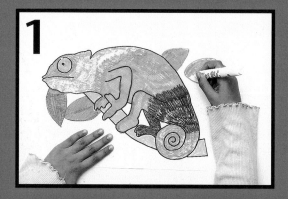

1

Colour in one of the chameleon pictures in shades of green and blue. Use oranges and purples for the second chameleon picture.

You will need
- 2 pieces of A4 paper, each with an outline of a chameleon on it
- Multi-coloured felt-tip pens
- Ruler
- Pencil
- Scissors
- A piece of paper that measures at least 21 by 60 centimetres
- Glue

2

Finish adding backgrounds to both pictures. Using a ruler and pencil, draw lines down both pictures at intervals of three centimetres.

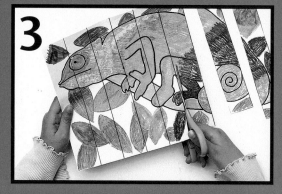

3

Carefully cut along the lines, so that your pictures are in long, thin strips. Pile them in order, with the chameleon head on top.

4 Take the long piece of paper. Glue the top strip of the green picture on the left. Next to it, paste the first strip of the purple picture. Carry on like this until there are no strips left. When dry, fold the new picture along the joins, into a zig-zag shape.

Look at the picture from the right and you see the green chameleon.

Look at it from the left and there is the purple chameleon.

Glossary

Algae – tiny plant-like organisms

Blend – to mix in with the surroundings

Cells – tiny units from which all living things are made

Cloud forest – a tropical mountain rainforest

Coat – the skin and fur of a mammal

Dappled – patterned with spots or patches of a darker colour

Decoy – something which is designed to mislead

Earthy – brown

Faint – to collapse or pass out

Glow – to shine brightly

Habitat – the area where an animal or plant lives

Inflated – blown up, like a balloon

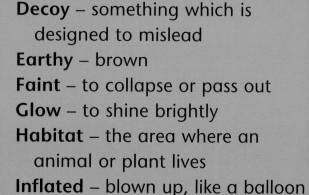

Larva – the young stage of some animals' lives

Lichen – a plant-like organism, made of a fungus and algae

Lure – an attractive-looking trap

Mimic – to copy

Mottled – a pattern of coloured blotches or stripes

Predator – an animal that hunts other animals for food

Prey – an animal that is hunted and killed by another animal

Savannah – stretches of dry grassland in tropical areas

Seabed – the bottom of the sea or ocean, usually covered with sand, rocks and stones

Sensitive – easily damaged

Shoal – a large group of fish swimming together

Startled – surprised

Tropical – an area near the equator with very hot weather

Venomous – poisonous

Visible – easy to see

This book includes material that would be particularly useful in helping to teach children aged 7–11 elements of the English and Science curricula, and provides opportunities for cross-curricular lessons involving Art.

Extension activities

Reading and writing
There are four different methods of camouflage: using colour (like the chameleon, pp26–27); mimicry of something else (like the crocodile, p20); disguise (like the crab on p29); and using colour and shape to blend in (like the zebras on p8). Find examples of each method from other parts of the book. Write a short report about one of them or create a table listing the key points about each method.

Writing
Write a fantasy story in which everything you see is an animal in disguise. Write clues describing an animal's disguise, such as 'It looks like a pile of dead leaves.' Can your friends identify the animal?

On page 32 there are animals that play tricks to escape predators. Write two accounts of an encounter between a predator and its prey, using their different viewpoints.

Look at the face painting on pages 44–45. Write and draw a set of instructions for a different design.

Speaking and listening
Make notes for a two-minute presentation comparing two animals in this book and their different methods of disguise.

Science
This book links with the themes of habitats (pp9, 10–11, 12–13, 14–15, 16–17, 18–19, 20–21, 22–23, 24–25, 28–29); life cycles (pp11, 13, 40–41); predation (pp6, 9, 12, 15, 18–19, 20, 27, 28, 30–31, 32–33, 34–35, 36–37, 38–39); and plants (pp16–17). On page 16 the text says animals help to spread plant seeds. Find out how this happens.

Cross-curricular links
1) *Art and design:* Look at the photograph of the hidden animal

on pages 18–19. Create a picture in which an animal hides in the landscape. Use collage or 3D techniques.

Look at pages 20–21. Gather some twigs and decorate them so that they look like stick insects. Put them together to make a display.

On page 22 are examples of countershading, where animals are disguised differently above and below. Design countershading to conceal an aeroplane, or a submarine. Draw your ideas onto templates.

Pages 30–31 feature different disguises using eyes. Create a picture of an animal that is decorated with false eyes.

Look at the turtle on pages 36–37. Design a picture of its head with a moving tongue, worked by tabs or levers.

2) Geography: Page 24 shows an Arctic habitat. Identify other habitats in this book and find their location in the world using a globe or atlas.

Using the projects
Children can follow or adapt these projects at home. Here are some ideas for extending them:

Pages 42–43: Find another animal that builds its disguise and make a model of that.

Pages 44–45: Paint a picture of an explorer who wants to blend in with the rainforest.

Did you know?

- There are over 3,000 different species of stick insect, found all over the world.

- The eggs of the stick insect are some of the largest in the insect kingdom – some reach over 8 millimetres long.

- The Arctic fox is the only member of the dog family that changes the colour of its fur.

- Every single zebra has a unique stripe pattern. Zebras identify each other this way.

- Balloon fish are not only dangerous because of their spikes and inflated bodies; they are among the most poisonous animals in the world. One fish contains enough poison to kill 30 people.

- The young of many mammals, such as lions and pigs, have camouflage markings. These disappear as the animals become older.

- Orchid mantises are born with black and orange bodies. Their colour changes as they grow older, depending on the colours in the environment around them.

- Not all camouflage is visual. Some animals roll around in the dung of other animals to disguise their own scent.

- A zebra's stripes make it easy to see when it's standing still, but when it's moving they create a blur which confuses predators.

- One type of caterpillar from Costa Rica frightens would-be attackers by mimicking a dangerous snake.

- Even some plants use camouflage: the 'living stone' plants found in African deserts look almost exactly like pebbles.

- The stomach of the hatchet fish glows with a light blue colour, the same colour as sunlight when it shines down into the ocean. This makes the hatchet fish nearly invisible to predators below it.

- Some hunters use scent to fool their prey. The bolas spider produces a scent similar to that of a female moth, which attracts male moths into its trap.

- Male chameleons often 'fight' each other by competing to show off their brightest colours.

Animal disguises quiz

The answers to these questions can all be found by looking back through the book. See how many you get right. You can check your answers on page 56.

1) Where do tapirs live?
   A – Deserts
   B – Rainforests
   C – Grassland

2) What colour is a zebra?
   A – Black and white
   B – Black and yellow
   C – Red and blue

3) Where do leopards like to rest on very hot days?
   A – In the river
   B – In long grass
   C – In leafy trees

4) Where do crab spiders sometimes catch their prey?
   A – On the seashore
   B – In tall trees
   C – In flowers

5) How does the stargazer fish camouflage itself?
   A – It buries itself in the seabed
   B – It hides behind bigger fish
   C – It looks like seaweed

6) How do chameleons change colour?
   A – They have special cells in their skin
   B – They shed their skin and grow a new one
   C – They rub themselves with green leaves

7) What colour is the Arctic fox in winter?
   A – Brown
   B – White
   C – Green

8) Where are the false eyes on a pearl-spotted owl?
   A – On its tail
   B – On its stomach
   C – On the back of its head

9) What is the body of the balloon fish covered in?
   A – Spots
   B – Spikes
   C – Stripes

10) Which animal uses a 'fishing line' to catch its prey?
    A – Anglerfish
    B – Fruit bat
    C – Praying mantis

11) What does the clearwing moth disguise itself as?
    A – An ant
    B – A crab
    C – A hornet

12) What do darkling beetles cover themselves in?
    A – Shells
    B – Lichen
    C – Leaves

Books to read

Animal Hide and Seek (DK Readers) by
Penny Smith, Dorling Kindersley, 2006
*Clever Camouflage (Animal Attack and
Defence)* by Kimberley Jane Pryor,
Macmillan Library, 2009
*Everything You Need to Know about
Animals* by Nicola Davies, Kingfisher,
2010
First Fun, Animal Encyclopaedia by Steve
Parker, Philip Steele, Jane Walker and
Brian Ward, Miles Kelly Publishing,
2005
The 10 Best Animal Camouflages by
Cameron Lindsey, Franklin Watts, 2008

Places to visit

The Natural History Museum, London
www.nhm.ac.uk
The Natural History Museum has a
number of exhibits showing animals
that use camouflage. It also has a very
extensive collection of insect specimens.

Birmingham Sealife Centre
www.sealife.co.uk
Take a trip down into the depths of the
ocean where you can see sea turtles,
sharks, butterfly fish, and various other
sea creatures.

Colchester Zoo
www.colchester-zoo.co.uk
Colchester Zoo has over 250 species of
animal to observe, including many that
use camouflage and feature in this book,
such as giraffes, zebras and tigers.

Edinburgh Zoo
www.edinburghzoo.org.uk
Edinburgh Zoo is Scotland's premier
animal conservation centre, housing
over 1,000 rare and endangered
animals. The zoo has a number of
visitor attractions including 'hands on'
sessions with the animals, keeper talks
and hilltop safari rides.

Websites

www.nhm.ac.uk
This website from the Natural History
Museum in London has several articles
on animals that use camouflage and
disguise to hide from predators and to
catch prey. It also has lots of other
information on the animal kingdom.

www.bbc.co.uk/nature/animals/
On this website you can find out all
about your favourite animals: the habitat
they live in, what they eat and how they
survive. There are also video clips for
each animal from BBC programmes.

www.animalcorner.co.uk
This website has information about a
wide variety of animals from all around
the world; it has also has a large number
of photographs as well as a fun activities
section for children.

Animal disguises
quiz answers

1) B   7) B
2) A   8) C
3) C   9) B
4) C   10) A
5) A   11) C
6) A   12) B